My Keto Lifestyle

Keto Diet Meal Plan For A Rapid Weight Loss

BY

NOVA BROWN

TABLE OF CONTENTS

INTRODUCTION

There are five varieties of the Ketogenic Keto diet, which have been distributed in restorative writing as successful medicines for ailments that have a hidden metabolic dysregulation, for example, epilepsy, disease, and Alzheimer's. The first Ketogenic Therapy, known as the typical Ketogenic Keto diet, or great Keto for short, was planned in 1923 by Dr. Russell for the treatment of epilepsy. All Ketogenic Keto diets are a variety of exemplary Keto, which is the most severe, seen by it's the proportion of fat to protein and carbs, additionally called the macronutrient proportion. Great Keto conveys a 4:1 balance, which infers that there are four areas fat for every one segment protein and carb. Since fat has a high caloric substance versus protein and carb (fat has nine calories for each gram, while both protein and carb have just four calories for every gram), 90% of calories originate from fat in a typical Ketogenic Keto diet. In contrast, 6% originate from protein, and 4% originate from the carb. The principle distinction between the five types of Ketogenic Keto diets is this macronutrient proportion.

All Ketogenic Keto diets are high in fat, sufficient in protein, and low in starches. This mix changes how vitality is utilized in the body, changing over fat into unsaturated fats and ketones in the liver. When there is a raised degree of ketones in the blood, one is in a condition of ketosis, which has a statement of practical advantages for the debilitated and sounds the same. Notwithstanding the macronutrient proportion, the recurrence of eating can impact ketosis. All the more explicitly, a training called discontinuous fasting, which diminishes the window of time individual eats for the day, can help in getting and continuing ketosis. At the point when the eating window is abbreviated, the body is compelled to get to vitality from its fat stores as opposed to calories legitimately from the eating regimen.

Ketogenic treatment incorporates something other than the keto diet. Healthful enhancements, electrolytes, hydration, and action levels are likewise key. People who are experiencing stomach related issues, for the most part, need extra help. This is the place an accomplished ketogenic pro can be amazingly useful. Checking ketosis is another significant part of treatment. Ketosis can be estimated by three unique techniques: Blood, breath, and pee. Blood readings are the most precise and dependable technique for testing. However, it is, likewise, the costliest. Pee strips give a reasonable choice. However, readings can shift broadly dependent on hydration. Breath screens have comparatively differing outcomes, and a higher section cost, yet, innovation is improving.

Think the ketogenic keto diet is directly for you? Converse with your primary care physician before receiving a ketogenic keto diet, or interface with one of our certified eating regimen experts to decide a game-plan that is directly for you.

DELICIOUS CAULIFLOWER

Total Time

Prep/Total Time: 30 min.

Makes

8 servings

Ingredients:

- 1 huge head cauliflower, broken into 1-inch florets (around 9 cups)
- 2 tablespoons olive oil
- 1 teaspoon smoked paprika

- 3/4 teaspoon salt
- 2 garlic cloves, minced
- 2 tablespoons minced new parsley

Directions:

1. Spot cauliflower in an enormous bowl. Consolidate the oil, paprika, and salt. Shower over cauliflower; hurl to cover. Move to a 15x10x1-in. Preparing container. Prepare, revealed, at 450° for 10 minutes.

2. Mix in garlic. Prepare 14 minutes longer or until cauliflower is delicate and daintily cooked, mixing every so often. Sprinkle with parsley.

SPICE TRADE BEANS AND BULGUR

© Viviane Matta

Total Time

Prep: 30 min. Cook: 3-1/2 hours

Makes

10 servings

Ingredients:

- 3 tablespoons canola oil, isolated
- 2 medium onions, slashed
- 1 medium sweet red pepper, slashed
- 5 garlic cloves, minced

- 1 tablespoon ground cumin
- 1 tablespoon paprika
- 2 teaspoons ground ginger
- 1 teaspoon pepper
- 1/2 teaspoon ground cinnamon
- 1/2 teaspoon cayenne pepper
- 1-1/2 cups bulgur
- 1 can (28 ounces) squashed tomatoes
- 1 can (14-1/2 ounces) diced tomatoes, undrained
- 1 container (32 ounces) vegetable juices
- 2 tablespoons darker sugar
- 2 tablespoons soy sauce
- 1 can (15 ounces) garbanzo beans or chickpeas, flushed and depleted
- 1/2 cup brilliant raisins
- Minced crisp cilantro, discretionary

Directions:

1. In a large skillet, heat 2 tablespoons oil over medium-high warmth. Include onions and pepper; cook and mix until delicate, 3-4 minutes. Include garlic and seasonings; cook brief longer. Move to a 5-qt. slow cooker.

2. In the same skillet, heat remaining oil over medium-high warmth. Include bulgur; cook and mix until

daintily caramelized, 2-3 minutes or until softly sautéed.

3. Include bulgur, tomatoes, stock, darker sugar, and soy sauce to slow cooker. Cook, secured, on low 3-4 hours or until bulgur is delicate. Mix in beans and raisins; cook 30 minutes longer. Whenever wanted, sprinkle with cilantro.

TOFU CHOW MEIN

Total Time
Prep: 15 min. + standing Cook: 15 min.
Makes
4 servings
Ingredients:

- 8 ounces uncooked entire wheat holy messenger hair pasta
- 3 tablespoons sesame oil, separated
- 1 bundle (16 ounces) extra-firm tofu
- 2 cups cut new mushrooms
- 1 medium sweet red pepper, julienned

- 1/4 cup decreased sodium soy sauce
- 3 green onions daintily cut

Directions:

1. Cook pasta as per bundle headings. Channel; flush with cold water and channel once more. Hurl with 1 tablespoon oil; spread onto a preparing sheet and let remain around 60 minutes.
2. In the meantime, cut tofu into 1/2-in. 3D shapes and smudge dry. Enclose by a clean kitchen towel; place on a plate and refrigerate until prepared to cook.
3. In an enormous skillet, heat 1 tablespoon oil over medium warmth. Include pasta, spreading equitably; cook until the base is daintily caramelized, around 5 minutes. Expel from skillet.
4. In the same skillet, heat remaining oil over medium-high warmth; pan sear mushrooms, pepper, and tofu until mushrooms are delicate, 3-4 minutes. Include pasta and soy sauce; hurl and heat through. Sprinkle with green onions.

CHARD AND WHITE BEAN PASTA

Total Time

Prep: 20 min. Cook: 20 min.

Makes

8 servings

Ingredients:

- 1 bundle (12 ounces) uncooked entire wheat or darker rice penne pasta
- 2 tablespoons olive oil
- 4 cups cut leeks (a white bit as it were)
- 1 cup cut sweet onion

- 4 garlic cloves, cut
- 1 tablespoon minced crisp savvy or 1 teaspoon scoured sage
- 1 enormous sweet potato, stripped and cut into 1/2-inch solid shapes
- 1 medium bundle Swiss chard (around 1 pound), cut into 1-inch cuts
- 1 can (15-1/2 ounces) extraordinary northern beans, flushed and depleted
- 3/4 teaspoon salt
- 1/4 teaspoon bean stew powder
- 1/4 teaspoon squashed red pepper drops
- 1/8 teaspoon ground nutmeg
- 1/8 teaspoon pepper
- 1/3 cup finely slashed crisp basil
- 1 tablespoon balsamic vinegar
- 2 cups marinara sauce, warmed

Directions:

1. Cook pasta as indicated by bundle headings. Channel, holding 3/4 cup pasta water.
2. In a 6-qt. stockpot, heat oil over medium warmth; saute leeks and onion until delicate, 5-7 minutes. Include garlic and sage; cook and mix 2 minutes.
3. Include potato and chard; cook, secured, over medium-low warmth 5 minutes. Mix in beans,

seasonings and held pasta water; cook, secured, until potato and chard are delicate, around 5 minutes.

4. Include pasta, basil, and vinegar; hurl and warmth through. Present with sauce.

OKRA ROASTED WITH SMOKED PAPRIKA

Total Time

Prep: 5 min. Cook: 30 min.

Makes

12 servings

Ingredients:

- 3 pounds new okra cases
- 3 tablespoons olive oil
- 3 tablespoons lemon juice

- 1-1/2 teaspoons smoked paprika
- 1/4 teaspoon garlic powder
- 3/4 teaspoon salt
- 1/2 teaspoon pepper

Directions:

1. Preheat stove to 400°. Hurl together all fixings. Mastermind in a 15x10x1-in. Heating skillet; cook until okra is delicate and softly sautéed, 30-35 minutes.

GARDEN VEGETABLE AND HERB SOUP

Total Time

Prep: 20 min. Cook: 30 min.

Makes

8 servings (2 quarts)

Ingredients:

- 2 tablespoons olive oil

- 2 medium onions, hacked
- 2 huge carrots, cut
- 1 pound red potatoes (around 3 medium), cubed
- 2 cups of water
- 1 can (14-1/2 ounces) diced tomatoes in sauce
- 1-1/2 cups vegetable soup
- 1-1/2 teaspoons garlic powder
- 1 teaspoon dried basil
- 1/2 teaspoon salt
- 1/2 teaspoon paprika
- 1/4 teaspoon dill weed
- 1/4 teaspoon pepper
- 1 medium yellow summer squash, split and cut
- 1 medium zucchini, split and cut

Directions:

1. In a huge pan, heat oil over medium warmth. Include onions and carrots; cook and mix until onions are delicate, 4-6 minutes. Include potatoes and cook 2 minutes. Mix in water, tomatoes, juices, and seasonings. Heat to the point of boiling. Diminish heat; stew, revealed, until potatoes and carrots are delicate, 9 minutes.

2. Include yellow squash and zucchini; cook until vegetables are delicate, 9 minutes longer. Serve or, whenever wanted, puree blend in clusters, including extra stock until desired consistency is accomplished.

CAULIFLOWER WITH ROASTED ALMOND AND PEPPER DIP

Ingredients:

Total Time

Prep: 40 min. Bake: 35 min.

Makes

10 servings (2-1/4 cups dip)

Ingredients:

- 10 cups water
- 1 cup olive oil, isolated

- 3/4 cup sherry or red wine vinegar, isolated
- 3 tablespoons salt
- 1 cove leaf
- 1 tablespoon squashed red pepper drops
- 1 enormous head cauliflower
- 1/2 cup entire almonds, toasted
- 1/2 cup delicate entire wheat or white bread morsels, toasted
- 1/2 cup fire-simmered squashed tomatoes
- 1 container (8 ounces) broiled sweet red peppers, depleted
- 2 tablespoons minced new parsley
- 2 garlic cloves
- 1 teaspoon sweet paprika
- 1/2 teaspoon salt
- 1/4 teaspoon newly ground pepper

Directions:

1. In a 6-qt. stockpot, bring water, 1/2 cup oil, 1/2 cup sherry, salt, sound leaf and pepper pieces to a bubble. Include cauliflower. Diminish heat; stew, revealed, until a blade effectively embeds into focus, 15-20 minutes, turning part of the way through cooking. Evacuate with an opened spoon; channel well on paper towels.

2. Preheat broiler to 450°. Spot cauliflower on a lubed wire rack in a 15x10x1-in. heating dish. Prepare on a lower broiler rack until dim brilliant, 39 minutes.

3. In the meantime, place almonds, bread morsels, tomatoes, cooked peppers, parsley, garlic, paprika, salt, and pepper in a nourishment processor; beat until finely cleaved. Include remaining sherry; process until mixed. Keep preparing while step by step, including remaining oil in a constant flow. Present with cauliflower.

SPICY GRILLED BROCCOLI

Total Time
Prep: 20 min. + standing Grill: 10 min.
Makes
6 servings
Ingredients:

- 2 packs broccoli
- MARINADE:
- 1/2 cup olive oil
- 1/4 cup juice vinegar
- 1 teaspoon onion powder
- 1 teaspoon garlic powder
- 1 teaspoon smoked paprika
- 1/2 teaspoon salt
- 1/2 teaspoon squashed red pepper pieces
- 1/4 teaspoon pepper

Direction:

1. Cut every broccoli pack into 6 pieces. In a 6-qt. stockpot, place a steamer container more than 1 in. of water. Spot broccoli in a bushel. Heat water to the point of boiling. Decrease warmth to keep up a stew; steam, secured, 4-6 minutes or until fresh delicate.

2. In an enormous bowl, whisk marinade fixings until mixed. Include broccoli; delicately hurl to cover. Let stand, secured, 15 minutes.

3. Channel broccoli, saving marinade. Flame broil broccoli, secured, over medium warmth, or cook 4 in from heat 6-8 minutes or until broccoli is delicate, turning once. Whenever wanted, present withheld marinade.

SAUTEED SQUASH WITH TOMATOES AND ONIONS

Total Time

Prep/Total Time: 20 min.

Makes

8 servings

Ingredients:

- 2 tablespoons olive oil
- 1 medium onion, finely hacked
- 4 medium zucchini, hacked
- 2 huge tomatoes, finely hacked
- 1 teaspoon salt
- 1/4 teaspoon pepper

Directions:

1. In a huge skillet, heat oil over medium-high warmth. Include onion; cook and mix until delicate, 2-4 minutes. Include zucchini; cook and mix 3 minutes.
2. Mix in tomatoes, salt, and pepper; cook and mix until squash is delicate, 4-6 minutes longer. Present with an opened spoon.

EGGPLANT SAUCE

Total Time

Prep: 20 min. Cook: 1 hour.

Makes

5 servings (4 quarts)

Ingredients:

- 2 tablespoons olive oil
- 1 medium onion, finely hacked
- 4 medium zucchini, hacked
- 2 huge tomatoes, finely hacked
- 1 teaspoon salt
- 1/4 teaspoon pepper

Directions:

1. Attachment in the Instant Pot and press the "Sauté" work. Include the ground meat of decision to the tempered steel cooking addition and keep on carmelizing meat until never again pink. Evacuate the meat and cooking fluid and put it in a safe spot.

2. Include the olive oil and onions to the pot and sauté until they start to relax and turn translucent. Add a spot of salt to bring out flavors and discharge juices.

3. Add the eggplant to the pot. Keep sautéing until onions and eggplant are delicate.

4. Include the crushed garlic and cook for one moment until garlic is fragrant.

5. Include the ACV and join well. Give the vinegar a chance to cook off for a moment or two, blending always. Scrape up any darker bits appended to the base of the pot. On the off chance that the nourishment begins to darker also rapidly include a limited quantity of water or progressively olive oil to anticipate consuming.

6. Include the jar of tomato glue to the pot, mix well, and let the tomato glue cook off for a moment or two to relax the flavor.

7. Include the jar of murmured tomatoes, flavors, 1 tsp salt, new parsley and the ground meat (with any juices on the plate) and mix to consolidate, trailed by 1 cup water (or bone juices).

8. Press the "Keep Warm/Cancel" catch to stop the sauté mode.

9. Mix and afterward place the top on the Instant Pot and lock the cover. Wind the steam discharge handle on the cover to "Fixing".

More recipes:

1. Press the "Manual" catch to switch the cooking mode. Utilize the "+/ - " catches to set the cooking time to 15 minutes. Note that the sauce will cook for longer than

15 minutes as it requires some investment for the constrain cooker to arrive at the wanted weight. The brief clock will begin once the appropriate weight is accomplished.

2. When the sauce is finished cooking the Instant Pot will consequently change to the "Keep Warm" mode and will flag finished with blares. When you hear the blares, the soup has cooked for the full 15 minutes at total weight. Give the sauce a chance to stay in the "Keep Warm" mode for 10 minutes and afterward press "Drop."

3. Contort the steam discharge handle on the cover to "Venting". I generally put on my stove glove as a precautionary measure as a modest quantity of steam will escape from the venting opening.

4. When the weight has discharged, cautiously open the Instant Pot.

5. Test for flavoring. Include increasingly pink salt, crisp broke pepper and new crushed lemon juice to taste.

6. Appreciate with avocado pieces, crisp split pepper, and new lemon wedges or served over pasta, rice or spiralized veggies of decision.

SQUASH AND CORN CHOWDER

Nutritional Information

Serves	Preparation Time	Calories	Protein	Fat	Carbs
7	5	35g	27	6g	32g

Ingredients:

- 3 tablespoons extra-virgin olive oil

- 1 cup diced onion

- 1 cup diced celery

- ½ cup generally useful flour

- 1½ teaspoons dried marjoram

- ¼ teaspoon salt

- ¼ teaspoon ground pepper

- 4 cups decreased sodium chicken soup

- 1 cup entire milk

- 3 cups diced summer squash

- 2 cups diced red potatoes

- 1 cup of corn parts

- ¾ cup diced ham

- Cut scallions for decorate

- Shredded pepper Jack cheddar for decorate

Directions:

1. Heat oil in a large pot over medium warmth.

2. Include onion and celery; cook, blending as often as possible until mollified and starting to dark-colored, 5 minutes.

3. Sprinkle flour, marjoram, salt and pepper over the vegetables and cook, mixing, for brief more. Include soup and milk; bring to a delicate bubble, mixing continually.

4. Mix in squash, potatoes, and corn; carry just to a stew. Stew, revealed, mixing once in a while, until the potatoes are delicate, 14 minutes.

5. Include ham and cook, mixing much of the time, until warmed through, around 2 minutes.

6. Serve bested with scallions and cheddar, whenever wanted.

7. To make ahead: Cover and refrigerate for as long as 4 days, gradually warm over medium-low or microwave on Medium power.

8. Monday: Lunch

LEMON CHICKEN & RICE

Nutritional Information

Serves	Preparation Time	Calories	Protein	Fat	Carbs
3	8	50g	71	9g	37g

Ingredients:

- 2 tablespoons olive oil, separated

- 8 boneless, skinless chicken thighs (1¼-1½ lbs. complete), cut

- 2 big onions, meagerly cut

- ½ teaspoon salt, separated

- 3 cloves garlic, minced

- 2 teaspoons ground turmeric

- 1 teaspoon paprika

- A liberal squeeze of saffron (discretionary)

- 3 cups destroyed cabbage (about ½ little head)

- 4 cups cooked dark colored rice, ideally basmati or jasmine

- ¼ cup lemon juice

- 2 tablespoons slashed new Italian parsley (discretionary)

- 1 lemon, cut (discretionary)

Directions:

1. Preheat broiler to 375°F.
2. Coat two 8-inch-square preparing dishes or foil skillet with cooking splash.
3. Heat 1 Tbsp. oil in a huge nonstick skillet over medium-high warmth. Include 4 chicken thighs, and cook, turning once, until the two sides are softly caramelized, around 4 minutes.
4. Move the chicken to a plate and put it in a safe spot. Rehash with the staying chicken thighs.
5. Pour off everything except around 1 Tbsp. fat from the dish. Include the staying 1 Tbsp. oil and onions to the container and sprinkle with ¼ tsp. salt.
6. Cook, blending, until delicate and brilliant, 12 to 15 minutes. Mix in garlic, turmeric, paprika, and saffron, if utilizing; cook, combining, for 2 minutes. Move the onions to a plate and put it in a safe spot. Return the dish to medium-high warmth and include cabbage — Cook, mixing, until dried, around 3 minutes.
7. Mix in rice, lemon squeeze, the remaining ¼ tsp. salt, and half of the held onion. Keep cooking until the rice is all around covered and warmed through, 6 minutes.
8. Gap the rice blend between the readied heating dishes; settle 4 of the held chicken thighs in each dish.

Top each with half of the staying cooked onions. Spread the two plates with foil.

9. Mark one and stop for as long as multi-month. Heat the rest of the dish, secured, for 30 minutes. Reveal and keep preparing until a thermometer embedded in the thickest piece of the chicken registers 165°F and the onions are beginning to dark-colored around the edges, 5 to 10 minutes more. Topping with parsley and lemon cuts, whenever wanted.

CHEESY CHIPOTLE-CAULIFLOWER MAC

Nutritional Information

Serves	Preparation Time	Calories	Protein	Fat	Carbs
7	10	35g	71	40g	22g

Ingredients:

- 3 cups cauliflower florets
- 8 ounces entire wheat fusilli or rotini pasta
- 1 cup nonfat milk
- 1 chipotle pepper in adobo, minced, in addition to 1 tablespoon adobo sauce
- 1 tablespoon olive oil
- ¼ cup finely hacked yellow onion
- 2 cloves garlic, minced
- 4 cups hacked new spinach
- ¼ teaspoon salt
- 1 tablespoon entire grain Dijon mustard

- 4 ounces decreased fat cheddar, destroyed (around 1 cup)
- 2 ounces part-skim mozzarella cheddar, destroyed (about ½ cup)
- Ground pepper (discretionary)
- Paprika (discretionary)

Directions:

1. Spot a steamer crate in a huge pot, add water to simply underneath the container and heat to the point of boiling.
2. Add cauliflower to the bin; spread, diminish warmth to medium and steam until delicate, 8 to 10 minutes. In the interim, heat a huge pot of water to the point of boiling.
3. Cook pasta for 2 minutes, not precisely the bundle bearings. Channel the pasta and move to a huge bowl. Move the cauliflower to a nourishment processor or blender. Include milk, chipotle and adobo sauce; puree until smooth.
4. Dry the enormous pot. Include oil and warmth over medium warmth. Include onion and cook until relaxed and straightforward, 2 to 3 minutes. Include garlic and cook until fragrant, 1 moment. Include spinach and cook until gently withered, 2 minutes.

5. Reduce heat to medium-low, cautiously include the cauliflower blend and mix to join. Mix in salt and mustard. Slowly race in Cheddar and mozzarella just until smooth, around 1 moment.

6. Remove from heat. Pour the sauce over the pasta and tenderly mix to join. Embellishment with pepper and paprika, whenever wanted.

KETO DELICIUOS SOUP

Total Time

Prep: 20 min. Cook: 45 min.

Makes

8 servings

Ingredients:

- 1 bundle broccoli (around 1-1/2 pounds)
- 1 tablespoon canola oil
- 1/2 pound cut crisp mushrooms
- 1 tablespoon diminished sodium soy sauce
- 2 medium carrots, finely slashed
- 2 celery ribs, finely slashed
- 1/4 cup finely slashed onion
- 1 garlic clove, minced
- 1 container (32 ounces) vegetable juices
- 2 cups of water
- 2 tablespoons lemon juice

Directions:

1. Cut broccoli florets into reduced down pieces. Strip and hack stalks.
2. In an enormous pot, heat oil over medium-high warmth; saute mushrooms until delicate, 4-6 minutes. Mix in soy sauce; expel from skillet. In the same

container, join broccoli stalks, carrots, celery, onion, garlic, soup, and water; heat to the point of boiling. Diminish heat; stew, revealed, until vegetables are relaxed, 25-30 minutes. Puree soup utilizing a drenching blender. Or then again, cool marginally and puree the soup in a blender; come back to the dish. Mix in florets and mushrooms; heat to the point of boiling. Lessen warmth to medium; cook until broccoli is delicate, 8-10 minutes, blending infrequently. Mix in lemon juice.

AVOCADO FRUIT SALAD WITH TANGERINE VINAIGRETTE

Total Time

Prep/Total Time: 25 min.

Makes

8 servings

Ingredients:

- 3 medium ready avocados, stripped and meagerly cut
- 3 medium mangoes, stripped and meagerly cut
- 1 cup crisp raspberries
- 1 cup crisp blackberries
- 1/4 cup minced crisp mint
- 1/4 cup cut almonds, toasted

DRESSING:

- 1/2 cup olive oil
- 1 teaspoon ground tangerine or orange strip
- 1/4 cup tangerine or squeezed orange
- 2 tablespoons balsamic vinegar
- 1/2 teaspoon salt
  1/4 teaspoon naturally ground pepper

Directions:

1. Mastermind avocados and organic product on a serving plate; sprinkle with mint and almonds. In a little bowl, whisk dressing fixings until mixed; shower over a plate of mixed greens.

2. To toast nuts, prepare in a shallow container in a 350° stove for 5-10 minutes or cook in a skillet over low warmth until softly sautéed, mixing every so often.

GENERAL TSO'S CAULIFLOWER

Total Time

Prep: 25 min. Cook: 20 min.

Makes

4 servings

Ingredients:

- Oil for profound fat fricasseeing
- 1/2 cup generally useful flour
- 1/2 cup cornstarch
- 1 teaspoon salt
- 1 teaspoon preparing powder
- 3/4 cup club pop
- 1 medium head cauliflower, cut into 1-inch florets (around 6 cups)

SAUCE:

- 1/4 cup squeezed orange
- 3 tablespoons sugar
- 3 tablespoons soy sauce
- 3 tablespoons vegetable stock
- 2 tablespoons rice vinegar
- 2 teaspoons sesame oil
- 2 teaspoons cornstarch
- 2 tablespoons canola oil

- 2 to 6 dried pasilla or other hot chilies, cleaved
- 3 green onions, white part minced, green part daintily cut
- 3 garlic cloves, minced
- 1 teaspoon ground new gingerroot
- 1/2 teaspoon ground orange get-up-and-go
- 4 cups hot cooked rice

Directions:

1. In an electric skillet or profound fryer, heat oil to 375°. Consolidate flour, cornstarch, salt, and heating powder. Mix in club soft drink just until mixed (hitter will be slender). Plunge florets, a couple at once, into the player and fry until cauliflower is delicate and covering is light dark colored, 8-10 minutes. Channel on paper towels.

2. For the sauce, whisk together the initial six fixings; race in cornstarch until smooth.

3. In a huge pot, heat canola oil over medium-high warmth. Include chilies; cook and mix until fragrant, 2 minutes. Include a white piece of onions, garlic, ginger, and orange get-up-and-go; cook until fragrant, around 1 moment. Mix soy sauce blend; add to the pan. Heat to the point of boiling; cook and mix until thickened, 4 minutes.

4. Add cauliflower to sauce; hurl to cover. Present with rice; sprinkle with daintily cut green onions.

ROASTED CURRIED CHICKPEAS AND CAULIFLOWER

Total Time
Prep: 15 min. Bake: 30 min.
Makes
4 servings
Ingredients:

- 2 pounds potatoes (around 4 medium), stripped and cut into 1/2-inch solid shapes
- 1 little head cauliflower, broken into florets (around 3 cups)
- 1 can (15 ounces) chickpeas or garbanzo beans, flushed and depleted
- 3 tablespoons olive oil
- 2 teaspoons curry powder
- 3/4 teaspoon salt
- 1/4 teaspoon pepper
- 3 tablespoons minced crisp cilantro or parsley

Directions:

1. Preheat broiler to 400°. Spot initial 7 fixings in an enormous bowl; hurl to cover. Move to a 15x10x1-in. preparing containers covered with cooking shower.

2. Cook until vegetables are delicate, 30-35 minutes, blending every so often. Sprinkle with cilantro.

CHICKPEA MINT TABBOULEH

Total Time

Prep/Total Time: 30 min.

Makes

4 servings

Ingredients:

- 1 cup bulgur
- 2 cups of water
- 1 cup new or solidified peas (around 5 ounces), defrosted
- 1 can (15 ounces) chickpeas or garbanzo beans, washed and depleted
- 1/2 cup minced new parsley
- 1/4 cup minced new mint
- 1/4 cup olive oil
- 2 tablespoons julienned delicate sun-dried tomatoes (not stuffed in oil)
- 2 tablespoons lemon juice
- 1/2 teaspoon salt
- 1/4 teaspoon pepper

Directions:

1. In a huge pot, consolidate bulgur and water; heat to the point of boiling. Decrease heat; stew, secured, 10

minutes. Mix in crisp or solidified peas; cook, secured, until bulgur and peas are delicate, around 5 minutes.

2. Move to an enormous bowl. Mix in outstanding fixings. Serve warm, or refrigerate and serve cold.

CREAMY CAULIFLOWER PAKORA SOUP

Total Time

Prep: 20 min. Cook: 20 min.

Makes

8 servings (3 quarts)

Ingredients:

- 1 huge head cauliflower, cut into little florets
- 5 medium potatoes, stripped and diced
- 1 huge onion, diced
- 4 medium carrots, stripped and diced
- 2 celery ribs, diced
- 1 container (32 ounces) vegetable stock
- 1 teaspoon garam masala
- 1 teaspoon garlic powder
- 1 teaspoon ground coriander
- 1 teaspoon ground turmeric
- 1 teaspoon ground cumin
- 1 teaspoon pepper
- 1 teaspoon salt
- 1/2 teaspoon squashed red pepper chips
- Water or extra vegetable stock
- New cilantro leaves

- Lime wedges, discretionary

Directions:

1. In a Dutch stove over medium-high warmth, heat initial 14 fixings to the point of boiling. Cook and mix until vegetables are delicate, around 20 minutes. Expel from heat; cool marginally. Procedure in groups in a blender or nourishment processor until smooth. Modify consistency as wanted with water (or extra stock). Sprinkle with new cilantro. Serve hot, with lime wedges whenever wanted.

2. Stop alternative: Before including cilantro, solidify cooled soup in cooler compartments. To utilize, in part defrost in cooler medium-term. Warmth through in a pan, blending every so often and including a little water if fundamental. Sprinkle with cilantro. Whenever wanted, present with lime wedges.

VEGETABLE BROTH

Nutritional Information

Serves	Preparation Time	Calories	Protein	Fat	Carbs
8	10	315g	20	22g	32g

Ingredients:

- 4 medium tomatillos, husked, washed and coarsely hacked (8 ounces)

- ¼ cup hacked new cilantro

- 1 medium new jalapeño pepper, seeded and finely hacked (see Tip)

- 1 clove garlic, minced

- ¼ teaspoon salt, separated

- 1 (1¼ to 1½ pound) meat flank steak, 1 inch thick

- 1 teaspoon bean stew powder

- ¼ teaspoon ground cumin

- ¼ teaspoon garlic powder

- ¼ teaspoon ground pepper

- ¼ cup disintegrated queso fresco or ground Monterey Jack cheddar (1 ounce) (discretionary)

Directions:

1. For tomatillo salsa, consolidate the tomatillos, cilantro, jalapeño, garlic, and ⅛ teaspoon salt in a nourishment processor. Cover and procedure until the blend are slashed.

2. Put in a safe spot. Cut back excess from steak. Score the two sides of the steak in a jewel design; put in a safe spot. Mix together stew powder, cumin, garlic powder, ground pepper, and the remaining ⅛ teaspoon salt (see Tip) in a little bowl. Sprinkle uniformly over the two sides of the steak.

3. For a charcoal flame broil, place the steak on the barbecue rack legitimately over medium coals. Flame broil, revealed, for 17 to 21 minutes for medium (160°F), turning once part of the way through barbecuing. (For a gas flame broil, preheat the barbecue.

4. Spot the steak on the flame broil rack over the warmth. Cover and barbecue as coordinated.) Transfer the steak to a cutting board. Spread freely with foil; let represent 4 minutes.

5. Daintily cut the steak corner to corner over the grain. Present with the saved tomatillo salsa. Whenever

wanted, sprinkle with queso fresco (or Monterey Jack).

CHICKEN & BROCCOLI CASSEROLE

Nutritional Information

Serves	Preparation Time	Calories	Protein	Fat	Carbs
10	10	38g	20	7g	20g

Ingredients:

- 1 tablespoon canola oil

- 1 pound boneless, skinless chicken bosoms, cut

- ⅓ cup generally useful flour

- 4 cups decreased fat milk, separated

- 2 (9 ounce) bundles precooked dark colored rice

- 3 cups broccoli florets

- 1½ cups destroyed decreased fat sharp cheddar

- ½ teaspoon legitimate salt

- ½ teaspoon ground pepper

- ½ cup locally acquired firm seared onions

Directions:

1. Preheat stove to 400°F. Warmth oil in a huge ovenproof skillet over high warmth. Include chicken and cook until all-around seared, around 4 minutes for every side.

2. Move to a spotless cutting board and let it represent 5 minutes. Cut into 1-inch 3D shapes.

3. Whisk flour and ⅔ cup milk in a little bowl. Include the rest of the 3⅓ cups milk to the skillet; heat to the point of boiling over medium-high warmth — step by step speed in the flour-milk blend.

4. Come back to a bubble and cook, regularly mixing, until thickened, 2 to 3 minutes. Mix in rice and broccoli; come back to a bubble and cook until the broccoli is delicate around 2 minutes.

5. Mix in the chicken, cheddar, salt, and pepper. Sprinkle onions on top. Move the dish to the oven. Prepare until the dish is sautéed and foaming, 9 minutes. Let cool for 5 minutes before serving.

GREEK TURKEY BURGERS WITH SPINACH, FETA & TZATZIKI

Nutritional Information

Serves	Preparation Time	Calories	Protein	Fat	Carbs
7	15	30g	27	6g	32g

Ingredients:

- 1 cup solidified cleaved spinach, defrosted

- 1 pound 93% lean ground turkey

- ½ cup disintegrated feta cheddar

- ½ teaspoon garlic powder

- ½ teaspoon dried oregano

- ¼ teaspoon salt

- ¼ teaspoon ground pepper

- 4 little cheeseburger buns, ideally entire wheat, split

- 4 tablespoons tzatziki

- 12 cuts cucumber

- 8 thick rings red onion (about ¼-inch)

Directions:

1. Preheat flame broil to medium-high.

2. Crush abundance dampness from spinach. Consolidate the spinach with turkey, feta, garlic powder, oregano, salt and pepper in a medium bowl; blend well. Structure into four 4-inch patties.

3. Oil the barbecue rack. Flame broil the patties until cooked through and never again pink in the inside, 4 to 6 minutes for every side.

4. Assemble the burgers on the buns, beating each with 1 tablespoon tzatziki, 3 cucumber cuts, and 2 onion rings.

CHEESY SPINACH AND ARTICHOKE STUFFED SPAGHETTI SQUASH

Nutritional Information

Serves	Preparation Time	Calories	Protein	Fat	Carbs
20	12	35g	27	90g	32g

Ingredients:

- 1 (2½ to 3 pound) spaghetti squash, cut down the middle the long way and seeds evacuated

- 3 tablespoons water, isolated

- 1 (5 ounce) bundle infant spinach

- 1 (10 ounces) bundle solidified artichoke hearts, defrosted and slashed

- 4 ounces diminished fat cream cheddar, cubed and relaxed

- ½ cup ground Parmesan cheddar, isolated

- ¼ teaspoon salt

- ¼ teaspoon ground pepper

- Squashed red pepper and cut crisp basil for embellish

Directions:

1. Spot squash chop side down in a microwave-safe dish; include 2 tablespoons water. Microwave, revealed, on High until delicate, 10 to 15 minutes. (On the other hand, place squash parts chop side down on a rimmed preparing sheet.

2. Prepare at 400°F until delicate, 40 to 50 minutes.) Meanwhile, join spinach and the staying 1 tablespoon water in a huge skillet over medium warmth. Cook, mixing once in a while, until withered, 3 to 5 minutes. Deplete and move to an enormous bowl.

3. Position rack in the upper third of stove; preheat the oven. Utilize a fork to scratch the squash from the shells into the bowl. Spot the shells on a heating sheet. Mix artichoke hearts, cream cheddar, ¼ cup Parmesan, salt and pepper into the squash blend.

4. Divide it between the squash shells and top with the remaining ¼ cup Parmesan.

5. Cook until the cheddar is brilliant darker, around 3 minutes. Sprinkle with squashed red pepper and basil, whenever wanted.

PROSCIUTTO PIZZA WITH CORN & ARUGULA

Nutritional Information

Serves	Preparation Time	Calories	Protein	Fat	Carbs
10	15	40g	27	57g	22g

Ingredients:

- 1 pound pizza mixture, ideally entire wheat

- 2 tablespoons extra-virgin olive oil, isolated

- 1 clove garlic, minced

- 1 cup part-skim destroyed mozzarella cheddar

- 1 cup crisp corn bits

- 1 ounce meagerly cut prosciutto, attacked 1-inch pieces

- 1½ cups arugula

- ½ cup torn crisp basil

- ¼ teaspoon ground pepper

Directions:

1. Preheat barbecue to medium-high. Roll the mixture out on a daintily floured surface into a 12-inch oval.

2. Move to a delicately floured enormous preparing sheet. Join 1 tablespoon oil and garlic in a little bowl.

3. Bring the mixture, the garlic oil, cheddar, corn and prosciutto to the barbecue. Oil the flame broil rack

4. Move the outside layer to the barbecue. Flame broil the mixture until puffed and delicately caramelized, 1 to 2 minutes.

5. Flip the outside layer over and spread the garlic oil on it. Top with the cheddar, corn, and prosciutto.

6. Flame broil, secured until the cheddar is dissolved and the outside layer is delicately caramelized on the last, 4 minutes more.

7. Return the pizza to the preparing sheet. Top the pizza with arugula, basil and pepper. Shower with the staying 1 tablespoon oil.

CAULIFLOWER CHICKEN FRIED "RICE"

Nutritional Information

Serves	Preparation Time	Calories	Protein	Fat	Carbs
5	5	35g	220	122 g	32g

Ingredients:

- 1 teaspoon shelled nut oil in addition to 2 tablespoons, isolated

- 2 enormous eggs, beaten

- 3 scallions, meagerly cut, whites and greens isolated

- 1 tablespoon ground crisp ginger

- 1 tablespoon minced garlic

- 1 pound boneless, skinless chicken thighs, cut and cut into ½-inch pieces

- ½ cup diced red chime pepper

- 1 cup snow peas, cut and split

- 4 cups cauliflower rice (see Tip)

- 3 tablespoons decreased sodium tamari or soy sauce

- 1 teaspoon sesame oil (discretionary)

Directions:

1. Heat 1 teaspoon oil in a huge level bottomed carbon-steel wok or huge substantial skillet over high warmth. Include eggs and cook, without mixing, until completely cooked on one side, around 30 seconds.

2. Flip and cook until simply cooked through, around 15 seconds. Move to a cutting board and cut into ½-inch pieces.

3. Add 1 tablespoon oil to the skillet alongside scallion whites, ginger and garlic; cook, mixing, until the scallions have relaxed, around 30 seconds. Include chicken and cook, blending, for 1 moment.

4. Include ringer pepper and snow peas; cook, mixing, until simply delicate, 2 to 4 minutes. Move everything to an enormous plate.

5. Include the staying 1 tablespoon oil to the skillet; include cauliflower rice and mix until starting to relax around 2 minutes.

6. Return the chicken blend and eggs to the skillet; include tamari (or soy sauce) and sesame oil (if utilizing) and mix until very much joined — embellishment with scallion greens.

7.

COBB SALAD WITH HERB-RUBBED CHICKEN

Nutritional Information

Serves	Preparation Time	Calories	Protein	Fat	Carbs
11	20	35g	27	100g	40g

Ingredients:

Chicken

- 1 tablespoon extra-virgin olive oil
- 1 teaspoon garlic powder
- 1 teaspoon dried thyme
- ½ teaspoon dried oregano
- ½ teaspoon dried rosemary
- ½ teaspoon ground pepper
- ¼ teaspoon fit salt
- 2 (8 ounce) boneless, skinless chicken bosoms, cut
- **Vinaigrette**
- ⅓ cup extra-virgin olive oil

- ¼ cup lemon juice

- 2 teaspoons champagne vinegar

- ½ teaspoon legitimate salt

- ¼ teaspoon ground pepper

Plate of mixed greens

- 6 cups child kale

- 2 medium ready avocados, cut

- 2 huge hard-bubbled eggs, cut

- 2 cuts cooked bacon, disintegrated

- ½ cup disintegrated feta cheddar

- 10 strawberries, quartered

Directions:

1. Preheat flame broil to medium-high. To get ready chicken: Combine 1 tablespoon oil, garlic powder, thyme, oregano, rosemary, ½ teaspoon pepper, and ¼ teaspoon salt in a little bowl.

2. Rub the blend over chicken. Oil the barbecue rack. Flame broil the chicken until a moment read thermometer embedded in the thickest part enlists 160°F, 5 to 6 minutes for every side.

3. Move the chicken to a perfect cutting board and let rest for 10 minutes. Cut. To get ready vinaigrette: Whisk oil, lemon juice, vinegar, salt and pepper in a little bowl.

4. To gather serving of mixed greens: Arrange kale, avocados, eggs, bacon, feta, strawberries and the chicken on an enormous platter. Present with the vinaigrette.

SUPERFOOD CHOPPED SALAD WITH SALMON

Nutritional Information

Serves	Preparation Time	Calories	Protein	Fat	Carbs
15	30	80g	45	120 g	400g

Ingredients:

- 1 pound salmon filet
- ½ cup low-fat plain yogurt
- ¼ cup mayonnaise
- 2 tablespoons lemon juice
- 2 tablespoons ground Parmesan cheddar
- 1 tablespoon finely cleaved new parsley
- 1 tablespoon clipped new chives
- 2 teaspoons diminished sodium tamari or soy sauce
- 1 medium clove garlic, minced
- ¼ teaspoon ground pepper

- 8 cups cleaved wavy kale

- 2 cups cleaved broccoli

- 2 cups cleaved red cabbage

- 2 cups finely diced carrots

- ½ cup sunflower seeds, toasted

Directions:

1. Organize rack in the upper third of the oven. Preheat grill to high. Line a preparing sheet with foil. Spot salmon on the readied preparing sheet, skin-side down.

2. Cook, pivoting the dish from front to back once, until the salmon is obscure in the middle, 8 to 12 minutes. Cut into 4 segments.

3. In the meantime, whisk yogurt, mayonnaise, lemon juice, Parmesan, parsley, chives, tamari (or soy sauce), garlic and pepper in a little bowl. Join kale, broccoli, cabbage, carrots and sunflower seeds in a huge bowl. Include ¾ cup of the dressing and hurl to cover.

4. Gap the serving of mixed greens among 4 supper plates and top each with a bit of salmon and around 1 tablespoon of the rest of the dressing.

MACARONI WITH SAUSAGE & RICOTTA

Nutritional Information

Serves	Preparation Time	Calories	Protein	Fat	Carbs
12	21	32g	20	200g	20g

Ingredients:

- 2 tablespoons extra-virgin olive oil

- 6 tablespoons finely hacked yellow onion

- 6 ounces gentle pork wiener, housings expelled

- 1 14-ounce can no-salt-included entire stripped tomatoes, hacked, with their juice

- ¼ teaspoon ground pepper

- ⅛ teaspoon salt in addition to 1 tablespoon, partitioned

- 12 ounces slight cylinder molded pasta, for example, pasta al ceppo

- 6 tablespoons part-skim ricotta cheddar

- 10 crisp basil leaves, daintily cut

- ¼ cup naturally ground Parmigiano-Reggiano cheddar

Directions:

1. Put 2 quarts of water on to bubble in an enormous pot. In the interim, join oil, onion, and hotdog in a huge skillet over medium-high warmth.
2. Cook, mixing and disintegrating the hotdog with a spoon, until the onion is brilliant, 4 to 5 minutes.
3. Include tomatoes, pepper, and ⅛ teaspoon salt; cook until the tomatoes have diminished and isolated from the oil, 5 to 10 minutes.
4. Remove from heat. Include the staying 1 tablespoon salt to the bubbling water, mix in pasta and cook as indicated by bundle directions until merely delicate. Just before the pasta is done, return the sauce to medium-low warmth. Include ricotta and basil and mix until consolidated. At the point when the pasta is done, channel well and hurl with the sauce and Parmigiano. Serve without a moment's delay.

ASIAN BEEF NOODLE BOWLS

Nutritional Information

Serves	Preparation Time	Calories	Protein	Fat	Carbs
10	22	30g	21	202g	202g

Ingredients:

- 4 ounces dried multigrain high-protein spaghetti or rice noodles

- 2 tablespoons rice vinegar

- 2 tablespoons diminished sodium soy sauce

- 1½ tablespoons lime juice

- 1 tablespoon sesame oil

- 1 tablespoon canola oil

- 1 tablespoon nectar

- 1 tablespoon ground crisp ginger

- 2 cloves garlic, minced

- ¼ teaspoon salt

- ⅛ teaspoon squashed red pepper

- Nonstick cooking shower

- 12 ounces hamburger flank steak, cut and cut corner to corner into slender reduced down strips

- 1 cup cleaved English cucumber

- 1 cup destroyed red cabbage

- ½ cup slight reduced down strips carrot or bundled crisp julienned carrots

- 2 tablespoons destroyed crisp basil

- Lime wedges

Directions:

1. Cook pasta as indicated by bundle headings, discarding any salt; channel. Come back to skillet; cover and keep warm. In the meantime, for sauce, in a little bowl whisk together the following 10 recipes (through squashed red pepper).

2. Coat a 10-inch nonstick skillet with a cooking splash; heat over medium-high. Include meat, half at once, and cook 1 to 2 minutes or just until caramelized.

3. Remove from skillet. Lessen warmth to medium. Include ¼ cup of the sauce to skillet; cook 1 to 2 minutes or until fluid is almost vanished, mixing to scrape up hard darker bits.

4. Return meat with any juices; cook and mix 1 to 2 minutes more or until warmed through.

5. Separation pasta among unique dishes and shower with outstanding sauce. Top with meat, cucumber, cabbage and carrot and sprinkle with basil.

6. Top with extra basil, whenever wanted, and present with lime wedges.

SLOW-COOKER BRISKET SANDWICHES WITH QUICK PICKLES

Nutritional Information

Serves	Preparation Time	Calories	Protein	Fat	Carbs
7	6 hours	90g	20	200g	20g

Ingredients:

- 2 tablespoons smoked paprika
- 2 teaspoons genuine salt
- 1 teaspoon garlic powder
- 1 teaspoon onion powder
- 1 teaspoon coarsely ground pepper
- 3¼ pounds brisket, cut
- 1 tablespoon extra-virgin olive oil
- 1 16-ounce bottle rauchbier or 2 cups diminished sodium meat juices
- ½ cup white vinegar
- ½ cup juice vinegar

- 2 tablespoons light darker sugar

- 1 teaspoon pickling zest

- 1 teaspoon fit salt

- 2 pickling or smaller than expected cucumbers, cut

- 1 medium sweet onion, meagerly cut into rings

- 2 cloves garlic, slashed

- ½ teaspoon fit salt

- ½ cup low-fat mayonnaise

- 8 entire wheat buns

Directions:

1. To plan brisket: Combine paprika, salt, garlic powder, onion powder and pepper in a little bowl. Rub all over brisket.

2. Heat oil in an enormous, substantial skillet over medium warmth. Include the brisket and dark-colored the two sides, 3 to 5 minutes for every side. Move to a 6-quart moderate cooker.

3. Include lager (or juices) to the container alongside any residual flavor mix from your cutting board; increment warmth to high. Cook for 5 minutes, scraping up sautéed bits with a wooden spoon.

4. Pour over the brisket. Cover and cook on High for 6 hours or Low for 9 hours. To get ready pickles: Meanwhile, join white vinegar, juice vinegar and dark-colored sugar in a little pan; heat to the point of boiling over high warmth and cook for 1 moment.

5. Include pickling zest and 1 teaspoon salt. Fill an enormous, heatproof glass bowl and include cucumbers and onion.

6. Refrigerate, sometimes mixing, for in any event 1 hour or until prepared to serve. To plan garlic mayo: Mash garlic and ½ teaspoon salt into glue in a mortar and pestle or with the back of a spoon on a cutting board.

7. Consolidate the garlic blend with mayonnaise in a little bowl. Cover and refrigerate until prepared to serve. At the point when the brisket is done, move to a spotless cutting board and let rest for 10 minutes.

8. Maneuver the brisket separated into shreds with 2 forks and afterward coarsely hack the destroyed meat. Join the cleaved brisket with the fluid in the moderate cooker. To serve, channel the cured vegetables. Spread every bun with 1 tablespoon garlic mayo and top with about ¾ cup brisket and ½ cup pickles.

CHICKEN ENCHILADAS VERDES

Nutritional Information

Serves	Preparation Time	Calories	Protein	Fat	Carbs
6	45	90g	55	232g	70g

Ingredients:

- ¼ cup universally handy flour

- 1 cup unsalted chicken juices, isolated

- 2 cups tomatillo salsa

- 1 teaspoon ground cumin

- ½ cup slashed crisp cilantro, isolated

- 3 cups destroyed cooked chicken bosom

- 1 (15 ounces) can no-salt-included dark beans, flushed

- 3 ounces diminished fat cream cheddar

- 12 (5 inch) corn tortillas

- ½ cup destroyed Mexican cheddar mix

- ½ cup slashed tomato

- 6 tablespoons diminished harsh fat cream

Directions:

1. Preheat grill to 425°F. Whisk flour and ½ cup juices in a little bowl. Join the remaining ½ cup stock, salsa, and cumin in a medium pot. Heat to the point of boiling and race in the flour blend.

2. Cook over medium warmth, mixing once in a while until decreased to about 2½ cups, 6 to 8 minutes.

3. Mix in ¼ cup cilantro. Spread ½ cup of the salsa blend in a 9-by-13-inch ovenproof preparing dish. Join chicken, beans, cream cheddar and ½ cup of the salsa blend in an enormous bowl.

4. Spoon ¼ cup of the chicken blend onto the focal point of every tortilla and fold it up into a stogie shape.

5. Organize, crease side down, in a solitary layer over the salsa blend in the heating dish. Top the enchiladas with the rest of the salsa blend.

6. Heat until rising, around 15 minutes. Expel from broiler; increment stove temperature to sear. Sprinkle the enchiladas with cheddar.

7. Cook 8 creeps from the warmth source until the cheddar are dissolved 2 to 3 minutes. Top with tomato and the remaining ¼ cup cilantro and present with harsh cream.

CHICKPEA CURRY (CHHOLE)

Nutritional Information

Serves	Preparation Time	Calories	Protein	Fat	Carbs
8	22	12g	40	400g	200g

Ingredients:

- 1 medium serrano pepper, cut into thirds

- 4 enormous cloves garlic

- 1 2-inch piece crisp ginger, stripped and coarsely hacked

- 1 medium yellow onion, hacked (1-inch)

- 6 tablespoons canola oil or grapeseed oil

- 2 teaspoons ground coriander

- 2 teaspoons ground cumin

- ½ teaspoon ground turmeric

- 2¼ cups no-salt-included canned diced tomatoes with their juice (from a 28-ounce can)

- ¾ teaspoon legitimate salt

- 2 15-ounce jars chickpeas, washed

- 2 teaspoons garam masala

- New cilantro for decorating

Directions:

1. Heartbeat serrano, garlic and ginger in a nourishment processor until minced. Scratch down the sides and heartbeat once more. Include onion; beat until finely cleaved, however not watery.
2. Heat oil in a huge pot over medium-high warmth.
3. Include the onion blend and cook, mixing once in a while, until mellowed, 3 to 5 minutes. Include

coriander, cumin and turmeric and cook, blending, for 2 minutes.

4. Heartbeat tomatoes in the nourishment processor until finely slashed. Add to the skillet alongside salt. Diminish warmth to keep up a stew and cook, sometimes mixing for 5 minutes. Include chickpeas and garam masala, diminish warmth to a delicate casserole, cover, and cook, blending at times, for 7 minutes more.

5. Serve beat with cilantro, whenever wanted.

QUICK SHRIMP PUTTANESCA

Nutritional Information

Serves	Preparation Time	Calories	Protein	Fat	Carbs
12	35	32g	20	400g	250g

Ingredients:

- 8 ounces refrigerated crisp linguine noodles, ideally entire wheat

- 1 tablespoon extra-virgin olive oil

- 1 pound stripped and deveined enormous shrimp

- 1 (15 ounces) can no-salt-included tomato sauce

- 1¼ cups solidified quartered artichoke hearts, defrosted (8 ounces)

- ¼ cup slashed set Kalamata olives

- 1 tablespoon escapades, washed

- ¼ teaspoon salt

Directions:

1. Heat an enormous pot of water to the point of boiling. Cook linguine as per bundle guidelines.

2. Channel. In the interim, heat oil in a huge skillet over high warmth. Include shrimp in a solitary layer and cook, undisturbed, until sautéed on the last, 2 to 3 minutes.

3. Mix in tomato sauce. Include artichoke hearts, olives, escapades, and salt; cook, frequently blending, until the shrimp is cooked through and the artichoke hearts are hot, 2 to 3 minutes longer.

4. Add the depleted noodles to the sauce and mix it to consolidate. Partition among 4 pasta bowls serve hot.

CREAMY WHITE CHILI WITH CREAM CHEESE

Nutritional Information

Serves	Preparation Time	Calories	Protein	Fat	Carbs
8	22	32g	20	200g	120g

Ingredients:

- 2 (15 ounces) jars no-salt-included incredible northern beans, flushed, isolated

- 1 tablespoon canola oil

- 1 pound boneless, skinless chicken thighs, cut and cut into scaled-down pieces

- 1½ cups hacked yellow onion (1 medium)

- ¾ cup hacked celery (2 medium stalks)

- 5 cloves garlic, hacked (2 tablespoons)

- 1 teaspoon ground cumin

- ¼ teaspoon salt

- 3 cups unsalted chicken stock

- 1 (4 ounces) can hack green chiles

- 4 ounces decreased fat cream cheddar

- ½ cup approximately pressed crisp cilantro leaves

Directions:

1. Crush 1 cup beans in a little bowl with a whisk or potato masher. Warmth oil in an enormous substantial pot over high warmth.

2. Include chicken; cook, turning once in a while, until seared, 4 to 5 minutes. Include onion, celery, garlic, cumin, and salt. Cook until the onion is translucent and delicate, 6 minutes. Include the staying entire beans, the squashed beans, stock, and chiles. Heat to the point of boiling.

3. Reduce heat to medium and stew until the chicken is cooked through, around 3 minutes.

4. Remove from heat; mix in cream cheddar until dissolved. Serve bested with cilantro.

MINI MEATLOAVES WITH GREEN BEANS AND POTATOES

Nutritional Information

Serves	Preparation Time	Calories	Protein	Fat	Carbs
10	21	32g	20	300g	70g

Ingredients:

- ½ teaspoon paprika

- ½ teaspoon garlic powder, separated

- ¾ teaspoon salt, separated

- ¾ teaspoon ground pepper, separated

- 1 pound Yukon Gold or red potatoes, scoured and cut into 1-inch wedges

- 2 tablespoons extra-virgin olive oil, separated

- 1 pound lean (90% or less fatty) ground hamburger

- 1 huge egg, gently beaten

- ¼ cup finely hacked onion

- ¼ cup Italian-prepared panko breadcrumbs

- 3 tablespoons ketchup, separated

- 1 tablespoon Worcestershire sauce

- 1 pound green beans, cut

Directions:

1. Position racks in upper and lower thirds of the stove; preheat to 425°F. Coat 2 large rimmed heating sheets with cooking shower. Join paprika and ¼ teaspoon every garlic powder, salt, and pepper in a huge bowl. Add potatoes and hurl to cover.

2. Sprinkle with 1 tablespoon oil, hurl once more, at that point spread the potatoes in a solitary layer on one of the readied preparing sheets. (Hold the bowl.) Place on the lower rack to broil for 10 minutes.

3. Then, join meat, egg, onion, breadcrumbs, 2 tablespoons ketchup, Worcestershire and ¼ teaspoon every garlic powder, salt, and pepper in the enormous bowl. Structure the blend into 4 little portions around 2 by 4 inches each and place on the other arranged heating sheet.

4. Brush the tops with the staying 1 tablespoon ketchup. Remove the potatoes from the broiler and put the meatloaves on the lower rack. Hurl green beans with

the staying 1 tablespoon oil and ¼ teaspoon each salt and pepper.

5. Move the potatoes to the other side of their skillet and add the green beans to the opposite side.

6. Cook the vegetables on the upper rack until the green beans are delicate and a moment perused thermometer embedded into the focal point of the meatloaves registers 165°F, 25 minutes more.

SALMON-STUFFED AVOCADOS

Nutritional Information

Serves	Preparation Time	Calories	Protein	Fat	Carbs
11	22	32g	202	300g	210g

Ingredients:

- ½ cup nonfat plain Greek yogurt

- ½ cup diced celery

- 2 tablespoons cleaved crisp parsley

- 1 tablespoon lime juice

- 2 teaspoons mayonnaise

- 1 teaspoon Dijon mustard

- ⅛ teaspoon salt

- ⅛ teaspoon ground pepper

- 2 (5 ounces) jars salmon, depleted, chipped, skin and bones expelled

- 2 avocados

  Hacked chives for decorate

Directions:

1. Join yogurt, celery, parsley, lime juice, mayonnaise, mustard, salt, and pepper in a medium bowl; blend well.

2. Include salmon and blend well. Divide avocados the long way and evacuate pits.

3. Scoop around 1 tablespoon tissue from every avocado half into a little bowl. Crush the scooped-out avocado tissue with a fork and mix it into the salmon blend.

4. Fill every avocado half with about ¼ cup of the salmon blend, mounding it over the avocado parts. Embellishment with chives, whenever wanted.

STETSON CHOPPED SALAD

Nutritional Information

Serves	Preparation Time	Calories	Protein	Fat	Carbs
12	50	322g	203	200 g	20g

Ingredients:

- ¾ cup of water
- ½ cup Israeli couscous (see Tips)
- 6 cups child arugula
- 1 cup new corn portions (from 2 ears of corn)
- 1 cup split or quartered cherry tomatoes
- 1 firm ready avocado, diced
- ¼ cup toasted pepitas
- ¼ cup dried currants
- ½ cup cleaved new basil
- ¼ cup buttermilk
- ¼ cup mayonnaise

- 1 tablespoon lemon juice

- 1 little clove garlic, stripped

- ¼ teaspoon salt

- ¼ teaspoon ground pepper

Directions:

1. Heat water to the point of boiling in a little pot. Include couscous, diminish warmth to keep up a delicate stew, cover, and cook until the water is assimilated 8 to 10 minutes.

2. Move to a fine-work filter and flush with cold water.

3. Channel well. Spread arugula on a serving platter. Include the couscous, corn, tomatoes, avocado, pepitas, and currants in improving lines over the arugula.

4. Consolidate basil, buttermilk, mayonnaise, lemon juice, garlic, salt, and pepper in a small scale nourishment processor or blender; beat until smooth.

5. Top the plate of mixed greens with the dressing just before serving.

ZUCCHINI NOODLES WITH AVOCADO PESTO & SHRIMP

Nutritional Information

Serves	Preparation Time	Calories	Protein	Fat	Carbs
5	29	799g	500	208 g	203g

Ingredients:

- 5-6 medium zucchini (2¼-2½ pounds aggregate), cut

- ¾ teaspoon salt, separated

- 1 ready avocado

- 1 cup stuffed crisp basil leaves

- ¼ cup unsalted shelled pistachios

- 2 tablespoons lemon juice

- ¼ teaspoon ground pepper

- ¼ cup extra-virgin olive oil in addition to 2 tablespoons, separated

- 3 cloves garlic, minced

- 1 pound crude shrimp, stripped and deveined, tails left on whenever wanted

- 1-2 teaspoons Old Bay flavoring

Directions:

1. Utilizing a winding vegetable slicer or a vegetable peeler, cut zucchini longwise into long, flimsy strands or strips. Stop when you arrive at the seeds in the center.

2. Spot the zucchini "noodles" in a colander and hurl with ½ teaspoon salt. Let channel for 15 to 30 minutes, at that point tenderly crush to evacuate any overabundance water.

3. Then, consolidate avocado, basil, pistachios, lemon juice, pepper and the remaining ¼ teaspoon salt in a nourishment processor. Heartbeat until finely hacked. Include ¼ cup oil and process until smooth. Warmth 1 tablespoon oil in a large skillet over medium-high warmth include garlic and cook, mixing, for 30 seconds.

4. Include shrimp and sprinkle with Old Bay; cook, blending once in a while until the shrimp is nearly cooked through, 3 to 4 minutes.

5. Move to an enormous bowl. Include the staying 1 tablespoon oil to the skillet.

6. Include the depleted zucchini noodles and delicately hurl until hot, around 3 minutes. Move to the bowl, include the pesto and tenderly hurl to join.

ROASTED SALMON WITH SMOKY CHICKPEAS AND GREENS

Nutritional Information

Serves	Preparation Time	Calories	Protein	Fat	Carbs
4	5	32g	1.1	100 g	800g

Ingredients:

- 2 tablespoons extra-virgin olive oil, partitioned
- 1 tablespoon smoked paprika
- ½ teaspoon salt, partitioned, in addition to a squeeze
- 1 (15 ounces) can no-salt-included chickpeas, washed
- ⅓ cup buttermilk
- ¼ cup mayonnaise
- ¼ cup cleaved crisp chives or potentially dill, in addition to additional for embellish
- ½ teaspoon ground pepper, separated
- ¼ teaspoon garlic powder
- 10 cups packed kale

- ¼ cup of water

- 1¼ pounds wild salmon, cut into 4 segments

Directions:

1. Position racks in the upper third and center of the oven; preheat to 425°F. Join 1 tablespoon oil, paprika, and ¼ teaspoon salt in a medium bowl. Thoroughly pat chickpeas dry, at that point hurl with the paprika blend. Spread on a rimmed heating sheet.

2. Prepare the chickpeas on the upper rack, mixing twice, for 30 minutes. In the interim, puree buttermilk, mayonnaise, herbs, ¼ teaspoon pepper and garlic powder in a blender until smooth.

3. Put in a safe spot. Warmth the staying 1 tablespoon oil in a large skillet over medium heat. Include kale and cook, blending once in a while, for 2 minutes. Add water and keep cooking until the kale is delicate, around 5 minutes more.

4. Remove from warmth and mix when there's no other option of salt.

5. Remove the chickpeas from the stove and push them to the other side of the dish — Spot salmon on the opposite side and season with the remaining ¼ teaspoon each salt and pepper.

6. Prepare until the salmon is simply cooked through, 5 to 8 minutes. Sprinkle the saved dressing on the salmon, embellish with more herbs, whenever wanted, and present with the kale and chickpeas.

SLOW-COOKER MEDITERRANEAN CHICKEN AND CHICKPEA SOUP

Nutritional Information

Serves	Preparation Time	Calories	Protein	Fat	Carbs
5	35	210g	400	100g	220g

Ingredients:

- 1½ cups dried chickpeas splashed medium-term

- 4 cups of water

- 1 huge yellow onion, finely hacked

- 1 (15 ounces) can no-salt-included diced tomatoes, ideally fire-broiled

- 2 tablespoons tomato glue

- 4 cloves garlic, finely slashed

- 1 cove leaf

- 4 teaspoons ground cumin

- 4 teaspoons paprika

- ¼ teaspoon cayenne pepper

- ¼ teaspoon ground pepper

- 2 pounds bone-in chicken thighs, skin evacuated, cut

- 1 (14 ounces) can artichoke hearts, depleted and quartered

- ¼ cup divided set oil-restored olives

- ½ teaspoon salt

- ¼ cup slashed new parsley or cilantro

Directions:

1. Channel chickpeas and spot in a 6-quart or bigger moderate cooker. Include 4 cups water, onion, tomatoes and their juice, tomato glue, garlic, cove leaf, cumin, paprika, cayenne and ground pepper; mix to consolidate. Include chicken.

2. Cover and cook on Low for 8 hours or High for 4 hours. Move the chicken to a spotless cutting board and let cool somewhat.

3. Dispose of narrows leaf. Include artichokes, olives, and salt to the moderate cooker and mix to join.

4. Shred the chicken, disposing of bones. Mix the chicken into the soup.

5. Serve bested with parsley (or cilantro).

PORK CHOPS WITH GARLICKY BROCCOLI

Nutritional Information

Serves	Preparation Time	Calories	Protein	Fat	Carbs
9	57	320g	200	800g	20g

Ingredients:

- 1½ pounds broccoli with stems, cut and cut into lances
- 6 tablespoons extra-virgin olive oil, isolated
- 1 cup panko breadcrumbs, ideally entire wheat
- ¼ cup ground Parmesan cheddar, in addition to additional for serving
- ¼ cup entire wheat flour
- 1 huge egg, delicately beaten
- (4 ounces) boneless pork slashes, cut
- ¾ teaspoon salt, isolated
- 1 teaspoon lemon juice
- 4 cloves garlic, meagerly cut

- ¼ teaspoon squashed red pepper

- 2 tablespoons red-wine vinegar

- Hacked crisp thyme for decorating (optional)

Directions:

1. Position rack in the upper third of stove; preheat grill to high. Line a rimmed heating sheet with foil. Hurl broccoli with 1½ tablespoons oil on the readied container and spread in an even layer.

2. Sear, blending once until burned in spots, around 10 minutes. Move to a bowl and put in a safe spot. Then, consolidate breadcrumbs and Parmesan in a shallow dish. Spot flour in another shallow dish and egg in a third shallow dish. Sprinkle pork with ¼ teaspoon salt, at that point dig in the flour, shaking off overabundance; dunk in the egg, allowing abundance to trickle off; and cover with the breadcrumb blend.

3. Heat 3 tablespoons oil in an enormous nonstick skillet over medium-high warmth. Include the pork and cook, turning once, until brilliant dark colored and a moment read thermometer embedded in the thickest segment registers 145°F, around 6 minutes all out.

4. Transfer to a plate and sprinkle with lemon juice. Tent with foil wipe the skillet clean. Include the rest of the 1½ tablespoons oil, garlic, and squashed red pepper

and cook over low warmth, mixing, until the garlic is sizzling around 3 minutes.

5. Remove from warmth and mix in vinegar and the remaining ½ teaspoon salt. Shower over the saved broccoli and hurl to cover. Serve the pork and broccoli with more Parmesan and thyme, whenever wanted.

ZUCCHINI LASAGNA

Nutritional Information

Serves	Preparation Time	Calories	Protein	Fat	Carbs
12	21	320g	20	220 g	240g

Ingredients:

- 3 huge zucchini (3 pounds), cut the long way into ¼-inch-thick strips

- 1 tablespoon extra-virgin olive oil

- 12 ounces lean ground meat

- 1 cup hacked onion

- 2 cloves garlic, minced

- 1 (28 ounces) can no-salt-included squashed tomatoes

- ¼ cup dry red wine

- 1 teaspoon dried basil

- 1 teaspoon dried oregano

- ¾ teaspoon salt

- ¼ teaspoon ground pepper

- 1½ cups part-skim ricotta

- 1 huge egg, daintily beaten

- 1 cup destroyed part-skim mozzarella cheddar, separated

- Hacked new basil for decorate

Directions:

1. Preheat stove to 400°F. Coat 2 huge heating sheets with cooking splash. Mastermind zucchini cuts in a solitary layer on the readied preparing sheets.

2. Cook until naturally delicate, around 20 minutes. In the interim, heat oil in a large skillet over medium-high warmth. Include meat and onion; cook, mixing and disintegrating with a wooden spoon until the

hamburger is seared, 6 to 8 minutes. Include garlic and cook for one more moment. Include tomatoes, wine, basil, oregano, salt, and pepper; bring to a stew.

3. Reduce heat to medium-low and cook, mixing at times, until thickened, around 8 minutes.

4. Consolidate ricotta and egg in a little bowl. Spread around 1 cup of the tomato sauce in a 9-by-13-inch heating dish. Top with one-fourth of the zucchini cuts and afterward 1 cup sauce.

5. Touch one-fourth of the ricotta blend over the top and sprinkle with ¼ cup mozzarella. Rehash to make 3 additional layers with the rest of the zucchini, sauce, ricotta blend and mozzarella.

6. Prepare until the sauce is rising around the edges, around 30 minutes. Let represent 10 minutes before serving and trimming with basil.

ROASTED CAULIFLOWER AND POTATO CURRY SOUP

Nutritional Information

Serves	Preparation Time	Calories	Protein	Fat	Carbs
10	17	120g	80	700g	120g

Ingredients:

- 2 teaspoons ground coriander
- 2 teaspoons ground cumin

- 1½ teaspoons ground cinnamon

- 1½ teaspoons ground turmeric

- 1¼ teaspoons salt

- ¾ teaspoon ground pepper

- ⅛ teaspoon cayenne pepper

- 1 little head cauliflower, cut into little florets (around 6 cups)

- 2 tablespoons extra-virgin olive oil, partitioned

- 1 enormous onion, cleaved

- 1 cup diced carrot

- 3 enormous cloves garlic, minced

- 1½ teaspoons ground crisp ginger

- 1 crisp red chile pepper, for example, serrano or jalapeño, minced, in addition to additional for embellish

- 1 (14 ounce) can no-salt-included tomato sauce

- 4 cups low-sodium vegetable juices

- 3 cups diced stripped chestnut potatoes (½-inch)

- 3 cups diced stripped sweet potatoes (½-inch)

- 2 teaspoons lime pizzazz

- 2 tablespoons lime juice

- 1 (14 ounces) would coconut be able to drain

- Slashed crisp cilantro for embellishing

Directions:

1. Preheat broiler to 450°F.
2. Consolidate coriander, cumin, cinnamon, turmeric, salt, pepper and cayenne in a little bowl.
3. Hurl cauliflower with 1 tablespoon oil in a huge bowl, sprinkle with 1 tablespoon of the zest blend and hurl once more. Spread in a solitary layer on a rimmed heating sheet.
4. Cook the cauliflower until the edges are caramelized, 15 to 20 minutes. Put in a safe spot. In the meantime, heat the staying 1 tablespoon oil in a huge pot over medium-high warmth.
5. Include onion and carrot and cook, frequently mixing, until beginning to darker, 3 to 4 minutes. Decrease warmth to medium and keep cooking, mixing regularly, until the onion is delicate, 3 to 4 minutes. Include garlic, ginger, chili and the rest of the flavor blend. Cook, blending, for brief more.
6. Mix in tomato sauce, scraping up any cooked bits, and stew for 1 moment. Include stock, potatoes, sweet potatoes, lime get-up-and-go, and squeeze.

7. Cover and heat to the point of boiling over high warmth. Lessen warmth to keep up a delicate stew and cook, mostly secured and blending every so often, until the vegetables are delicate, 35 to 40 minutes. Mix in coconut milk and the roasted cauliflower. Come back to a stew to warm through. Serve embellished with cilantro and chiles, whenever wanted.

CRISPY OVEN-FRIED FISH TACOS

Nutritional Information

Serves	Preparation Time	Calories	Protein	Fat	Carbs
20	1 hour -20	32g	100	900	420g

Ingredients:

- Cooking shower

- 1 cup entire grain oat chips

- ¾ cup dry entire wheat breadcrumbs

- ¾ teaspoon ground pepper, isolated

- ½ teaspoon garlic powder

- ½ teaspoon paprika

- ½ teaspoon salt, isolated

- ½ cup universally handy flour

- 2 enormous egg whites

- 2 tablespoons water

- 1 pound cod, cut into ½-by-3-inch strips (cut down the middle on a level plane, if thick)

- 2 tablespoons avocado oil

- 2 tablespoons unseasoned rice vinegar

- 3 cups coleslaw blend

- 1 avocado, diced

- 8 corn tortillas, warmed

- Pico de gallo

Directions:

1. Preheat broiler to 450°F. Set a wire rack on a preparing sheet; cover with cooking shower.

2. Spot oat chips, breadcrumbs, ½ teaspoon pepper, garlic powder, paprika, and ¼ teaspoon salt in a nourishment processor and procedure until finely ground. Move to a shallow dish. Spot flour in a subsequent shallow dish. Whisk egg whites and water together in a third shallow dish.

3. Dig each bit of fish in the flour, dunk it in the egg white blend and afterward cover on all sides with the breadcrumb blend.

4. Spot on the readied rack. Coat the two sides of the breaded fish with cooking shower. Prepare until the fish is cooked through and the breading is brilliant dark-colored and fresh around 10 minutes. In the meantime, whisk oil, vinegar and the remaining ¼ teaspoon each pepper and salt in a medium bowl.

5. Add coleslaw blend and hurl to cover. Gap the fish, coleslaw blend and avocado uniformly among tortillas. Present with pico de gallo, whenever wanted.

BROCCOLI-CHEDDAR-CHICKEN CHOWDER

Nutritional Information

Serves	Preparation Time	Calories	Protein	Fat	Carbs
12	21	332g	240	700g	220g

Ingredients:

- 3 tablespoons extra-virgin olive oil
- 1 cup diced onion
- 1 cup diced celery
- ½ cup generally useful flour
- 1 teaspoon dry mustard
- ¼ teaspoon salt
- ¼ teaspoon ground pepper
- 4 cups decreased sodium chicken stock
- 1 cup entire milk
- 3 cups hacked broccoli florets
- 2 cups diced Yukon Gold potatoes

- 1 pound boneless skinless chicken bosoms, cut into scaled-down pieces

- 1 cup destroyed cheddar, in addition to additional for embellish

- Finely diced red onion for embellish

Directions:

1. Heat oil in an enormous pot over medium warmth. Include onion and celery; cook, mixing much of the time, until relaxed and starting to darker, 3 to 6 minutes.

2. Sprinkle flour, dry mustard, salt and pepper over the vegetables and cook, blending, for brief more. Include soup and milk; bring to a delicate bubble, mixing continually.

3. Mix in broccoli and potatoes and carry just to a stew. Stew, revealed, blending at times until the potatoes are delicate, 12 to 15 minutes.

4. Include chicken and 1 cup Cheddar and cook, blending as often as possible, until cooked through, 4 to 6 minutes.

5. Serve bested with somewhat more Cheddar and red onion, whenever wanted.

CHICKEN AND SPINACH SKILLET PASTA WITH LEMON AND PARMESAN

Nutritional Information

Serves	Preparation Time	Calories	Protein	Fat	Carbs
10	45	321g	220	209g	209g

Ingredients:

- 8 ounces sans gluten penne pasta or entire wheat penne pasta
- 2 tablespoons extra-virgin olive oil
- 1 pound boneless, skinless chicken bosom or thighs, cut, if vital, and cut into reduced down pieces
- ½ teaspoon salt
- ¼ teaspoon ground pepper
- 4 cloves garlic, minced
- ½ cup dry white wine
- Squeeze and pizzazz of 1 lemon
- 10 cups cleaved new spinach

  4 tablespoons ground Parmesan cheddar, partitioned

Directions:

1. Cook pasta as indicated by bundle bearings. Deplete and put in a safe spot. In the interim, heat oil in a large high-sided skillet over medium-high warmth. Include chicken, salt and pepper; cook, sometimes mixing, until cooked through, 5 to 7 minutes.

2. Include garlic and cook, blending, until fragrant, around 1 moment. Mix in wine, lemon squeeze and pizzazz; bring to a stew.

3. Remove from heat. Mix in spinach and the cooked pasta. Cover and let remain until the spinach is withered.

4. Gap among 4 plates and top each presenting with 1 tablespoon Parmesan.

VEGAN MANGO ALMOND MILKSHAKE

Serves	Preparation Time	Calories	Protein	Fat	Carbs
2	4	311g	290	109 g	29g

Ingredients

- 1 ripe of mango, must be pulp

- 3/4 cup of almond milk, must be unsweetened

- Ice

Directions:

1. Put all the ingredients in a blender & blend until smooth.

   Drink immediately after preparation.

PEANUT BUTTER MOCHA ESPRESSO SHAKE

Ingredients

- 1/2 solidified banana
- 1 tablespoon nutty spread
- 1 tablespoon unsweetened cocoa powder
- 1/2 cup almond milk
- 1/2 cup solid fermented espresso, chilled
- 3/4 cup ice

Directions

1. Consolidate all fixings in a blender. Mix until smooth.

CHOCOLATE CHIP BANANA PANCAKES

Ingredients

- 1/2 cups date, pit expelled
- 1/2 cup nutty spread
- 1/2 cup antiquated moved oats

Directions

2. Line a 8x8 preparing dish with material paper. Put in a safe spot.

3. Spot the dates in a nourishment processor and procedure until generally hacked. Note: if dates are not sodden and clingy before being cleaved, absorb the entire dates warm water for around 10 minutes.

4. After the dates have been slashed, include the nutty spread and the oats. Heartbeat until just combined.Press the blend into the readied heating dish. Spot in the cooler until set, around 60 minutes.

5. Cut and serve. Store in the cooler.

PEANUT BUTTER MOCHA ESPRESSO SHAKE

Ingredients

- 1 enormous excessively ready banana, crushed
- 2 tablespoons coconut sugar
- 3 tablespoons coconut oil, liquefied
- 1 cup coconut milk
- 1/2 cups entire wheat flour
- 1 teaspoon heating pop

- 1/2 cup veggie lover chocolate chips, we utilized Enjoy Life Mini Chips

Directions

1. In an enormous blending bowl, consolidate the banana, sugar, oil, and milk. Blend well to join. Include the flour and heating pop, cautiously mix until simply joined. Be mindful so as not to over blend. Delicately overlap in the chocolate chips.

2. Gently splash a skillet with non-stick shower and warmth on medium warmth. Pour around 1/4 cup of the player into the dish. Cook around 3 to 4 minutes, or until hotcakes start to rise in the middle. Cautiously flip and cook for another 2 to 3 minutes. When cooked, expel flapjack from the skillet and rehash the procedure until all the hitter has been utilized. Oil the skillet varying with non-stick shower in the middle of cooking the hotcakes.

3. Serve hot, whenever wanted top with maple syrup, nectar, coconut margarine, new natural product, or your preferred jam!